TWISTERS

Bird Watch

Su Swallow
and Simona Dimitri

Evans

Bird
Watch

First published 2005
Evans Brothers Limited
2A Portman Mansions
Chiltern Street
London W1U 6NR

Text copyright © Evans Brothers Limited 2005
© in the illustrations Evans Brothers Limited 2005

British Library Cataloguing in Publication Data
Swallow, Su
        Bird watch. - (Twisters)
        1. Children's stories - Pictorial works
        I. Title
        823.9'14 [J]

ISBN-10: 0237530724
13-digit ISBN (from 1 January 2007) 9780237530723

Printed in China by WKT Company Limited

Series Editor: Nick Turpin
Design: Robert Walster
Production: Jenny Mulvanny
Series Consultant: Gill Matthews

"Let's go birdwatching,"
said Dad.

"We need binoculars...

...some lunch...

...and warm clothes."

Dad and Ben set off.

They walked a long way.

They sat in a hide...

They ate lunch...

...and listened. No birds.

"Let's go home," said Ben.

"No luck?" said Mum.

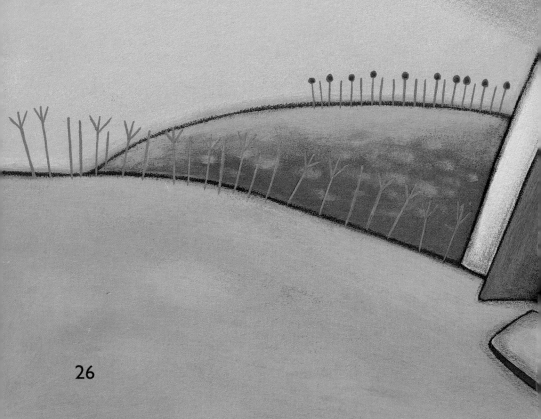

"Never mind. Look!"

"Birds!"